THE BIOGRAPHY

OF ROBERT

OPPENHEIMER

Unraveling the Mind behind the Atomic
Age

Lucas Jonathan

TABLE OF CONTENT

INTRODUCTION

In the tumultuous landscape of the 20th century, J. Robert Oppenheimer emerged as a towering figure, leaving an indelible mark on science, nuclear physics, and the course of world events. Born with an insatiable curiosity and a precocious intellect, Oppenheimer's journey through life was characterized by a relentless pursuit of knowledge, innovation, and the quest for truth.

His early fascination with literature and science foreshadowed the exceptional path he would follow. As a young physicist, Oppenheimer made groundbreaking contributions to theoretical physics, unraveling the enigmatic world of quantum mechanics and celestial processes. These intellectual feats positioned him as a leading mind in the scientific community, and soon, the world would bear witness to the magnitude of his capabilities.

In the crucible of World War II, Oppenheimer's life took an irrevocable turn. Leading the Manhattan Project, he became the orchestrator of the most momentous scientific endeavor in history. The successful development of the atomic bomb presented humanity with a dual-edged sword - an unprecedented source of power and destruction. The world was thrust into an era where scientific discoveries held the potential to alter the very fabric of existence.

Yet, the triumph of scientific progress came hand in hand with a profound ethical dilemma. As Oppenheimer stood witness to the devastating power of the atomic bomb unleashed upon Hiroshima and Nagasaki, his conscience wrestled with the ramifications of such technological prowess. He confronted the moral implications of scientific discovery, the thin line between the pursuit of knowledge and its unintended consequences on humanity.

In the aftermath of the war, Oppenheimer's life took on a new purpose. He advocated for arms control, emphasizing the importance of international cooperation to prevent nuclear proliferation and pave the way for peaceful uses of nuclear energy. Through his mentorship, he nurtured the minds of young scientists, instilling in them not only scientific brilliance but also a sense of responsibility to society.

Despite his towering intellect, Oppenheimer's life story was not immune to trials and tribulations. Controversies surrounding his political affiliations during the Second Red Scare led to the revocation of his security clearance, casting a shadow on his otherwise stellar career. The personal and professional challenges he faced served as a poignant reminder that human progress is not without its vulnerabilities and external pressures.

Beyond his scientific endeavors, Oppenheimer's life was an embodiment of multifaceted brilliance. His passion for literature, art, music, and philosophy painted a portrait of a man who cherished the rich tapestry of human expression. His ability to navigate multiple realms of knowledge showcased the profound interplay between the sciences and the arts, a testament to the interconnectedness of human learning.

Today, Oppenheimer's legacy endures as an enduring source of inspiration and reflection. His life story offers invaluable lessons on the ethical considerations of scientific research, the impact of scientific discoveries on society, and the quest for peaceful coexistence in a world shaped by technology.

As we journey through the complexities of the 21st century, the life of J. Robert Oppenheimer continues to beckon us to navigate the intertwining forces of science, ethics, and human aspirations. His brilliance and complexities serve as a guiding star, illuminating the path towards a future where scientific discovery is coupled with moral introspection and the human quest for knowledge is tempered by a profound responsibility to humanity.

CHAPTER 1

EARLY LIFE AND EDUCATION

OPPENHEIMER'S CHILDHOOD

J. Robert Oppenheimer was born on April 22, 1904, in New York City, into a privileged and intellectually stimulating environment. His childhood experiences and family background played a significant role in shaping his intellectual curiosity and laying the groundwork for his future achievements as a prominent physicist.

Oppenheimer's parents were both of Jewish descent and highly accomplished in their respective fields. His father, Julius Oppenheimer, was a wealthy textile importer and a successful businessman. His mother, Ella Friedman, came from a family of artists and intellectuals. Ella was a talented painter, and her family members were known for their intellectual pursuits, including literature and music.

From a young age, Oppenheimer displayed an insatiable curiosity about the world around him. He was a voracious reader and had a keen interest in literature, science, and art, likely influenced by the intellectual atmosphere of his home.

He attended the Ethical Culture School in New York City, where he was exposed to a progressive education approach that emphasized ethical and moral values alongside academic subjects. The school's emphasis on critical thinking and independent inquiry further nurtured Oppenheimer's inquisitive mind.

During his teenage years, Oppenheimer's interests gravitated toward science and literature. He immersed himself in classical literature, philosophy, and poetry, developing a broad intellectual base that would later influence his work as a scientist.

Oppenheimer's parents believed in providing their children with diverse experiences and sent him to summer camps, which further broadened his horizons. At these camps, he engaged in outdoor activities, including hiking and horseback riding, which instilled in him a love for nature.

One significant childhood experience that deeply impacted Oppenheimer was witnessing a solar eclipse. This event sparked his fascination with astronomy and the mysteries of the universe. Throughout his life, he would maintain a deep interest in astronomy and astrophysics, alongside his primary focus on quantum mechanics and theoretical physics.

Oppenheimer's parents recognized and encouraged his intellectual gifts, supporting his academic pursuits and providing him with the resources he needed to excel. They also introduced him to cultural activities, including visits to museums, concerts, and art exhibitions, which further enriched his intellectual growth.

OPPENHEIMER'S FAMILY BACKGROUND

J. Robert Oppenheimer came from a family with diverse and accomplished backgrounds. His family's intellectual and cultural influences played a significant role in shaping his interests and academic pursuits throughout his life.

Father - Julius Oppenheimer:

Julius Oppenheimer, J. Robert Oppenheimer's father, was a successful textile importer and businessman. He was born in Baltimore in 1866 and belonged to a well-off family of German Jewish immigrants. Julius's success in the textile industry allowed him to provide a privileged upbringing for his children, including J. Robert.

Mother - Ella Friedman:

Ella Friedman, J. Robert Oppenheimer's mother, was born in New York City in 1871. Her family background was marked by a strong inclination towards art and intellectual pursuits. Ella herself was a talented painter, and she had several artistically inclined family members, including her brother, who was a composer and music critic. Ella's love for art and culture had a profound impact on young Oppenheimer's early exposure to the arts.

Sibling - Frank Friedman Oppenheimer:

Oppenheimer had a younger brother named Frank Friedman Oppenheimer, born in 1912. Frank went on to become a respected scientist in his own right. He earned his Ph.D. in experimental physics from the University of California, Berkeley, and later became a professor at the University of Colorado Boulder. Frank was also involved in various educational initiatives and co-founded the Exploratorium, an interactive science museum in San Francisco.

Family Values and Support:

The Oppenheimer family emphasized education, culture, and intellectual exploration. They encouraged the pursuit of knowledge and supported their children's interests and endeavors. This nurturing environment played a crucial role in fostering J. Robert Oppenheimer's inquisitive mind and academic pursuits.

Jewish Heritage:

The Oppenheimer family was of Jewish heritage, and while they did not actively practice the Jewish faith, their ancestry was an important aspect of their identity. In the early 20th century, anti-Semitism was still prevalent in certain circles, and this may have influenced some of Oppenheimer's experiences throughout his life, especially during the McCarthy era when he faced accusations related to his associations with leftist organizations.

OPPENHEIMER'S EARLY INTERESTS IN SCIENCE AND LITERATURE

Oppenheimer's early interests in science and literature played a crucial role in shaping his intellectual development and approach to problem-solving throughout his life. His insatiable curiosity and exposure to diverse influences enriched his understanding of the world, fostering a multidisciplinary perspective that set him apart as a scientist and thinker.

Oppenheimer's early exposure to literature and poetry ignited a lifelong passion for the written word. He was captivated by the works of great writers and poets, delving into classics from various cultures and time periods. His love for literature provided him with a deeper understanding of human emotions, societal dynamics, and philosophical ideas. These insights influenced his scientific inquiries, as he sought connections between scientific principles and the human experience.

Oppenheimer's fascination with both science and literature led him to embrace an interdisciplinary approach to learning. He recognized the interconnectedness of various fields of knowledge and believed that a holistic education was essential for true intellectual growth. This multidisciplinary perspective allowed him to draw insights from seemingly unrelated subjects, leading to creative solutions in his scientific endeavors.

Attending the Ethical Culture School exposed Oppenheimer to discussions about ethics and social responsibility from a young age. These principles resonated deeply with him and influenced his approach to science and technology. Throughout his life, Oppenheimer remained mindful of the ethical implications of scientific discoveries, including his work on the atomic bomb. He wrestled with the moral dilemmas of using such powerful weapons and the potential consequences on humanity.

The Oppenheimer household was a hub of intellectual activity. Conversations about scientific breakthroughs, cultural developments, and social issues were commonplace. Oppenheimer's parents encouraged intellectual discussions and valued the pursuit of knowledge. Such an environment fostered his inquisitive nature and provided a strong foundation for his later achievements.

EDUCATIONAL JOURNEY

Oppenheimer's early education was influenced by his intellectually stimulating home environment and attendance at the Ethical Culture School. The progressive educational approach at this school emphasized critical thinking, ethics, and a multidisciplinary approach to learning, fostering Oppenheimer's early intellectual curiosity.

In 1922, Oppenheimer enrolled at Harvard University, one of the most renowned institutions in the world. Initially, he pursued a degree in chemistry, reflecting his early interests in the natural sciences. During his time at Harvard, Oppenheimer continued to explore his passion for literature and philosophy alongside his scientific studies.

As Oppenheimer delved deeper into his studies, he became more drawn to theoretical physics. Under the guidance of Professor Percy W. Bridgman, a Nobel laureate in physics, Oppenheimer shifted his academic focus from chemistry to physics. Bridgman recognized Oppenheimer's exceptional intellect and encouraged him to pursue his growing interest in theoretical physics.

At Harvard, Oppenheimer formed relationships with prominent physicists, including Harvey Hall, John Van Vleck, and Isidor Isaac Rabi. These connections provided him with valuable insights and opportunities to engage in cutting-edge research.

To further his education, Oppenheimer traveled to Europe, where he studied at the University of Cambridge and the University of Gottingen. At Cambridge, he attended lectures by renowned physicist Paul Dirac, whose groundbreaking work in quantum mechanics had a profound impact on Oppenheimer's understanding of the subject.

Oppenheimer's most significant educational milestone was his doctoral studies at the University of Gottingen in Germany. There, he worked under the guidance of renowned physicist Max Born, focusing on quantum mechanics and the application of quantum theory to atomic and molecular systems. In 1927, Oppenheimer earned his Ph.D. with a thesis on "Born-Oppenheimer Approximation," a significant contribution to quantum theory.

After completing his doctoral studies, Oppenheimer returned to the United States and took up positions at various institutions, including Harvard University and the California Institute of Technology (Caltech). He continued his research and collaborated with other leading physicists in the field.

CHAPTER 2

CAREER AND CONTRIBUTIONS TO PHYSICS

OPPENHEIMER'S RESEARCH WORK AND CONTRIBUTIONS TO THEORETICAL PHYSICS AND QUANTUM MECHANICS

J. Robert Oppenheimer made significant research contributions to theoretical physics and quantum mechanics, becoming one of the most influential physicists of the 20th century. His work spanned various areas of theoretical physics, and he played a key role in shaping our understanding of quantum mechanics and the behavior of subatomic particles.

One of Oppenheimer's early and most impactful contributions was the development of the Born-Oppenheimer Approximation. In his doctoral research at the University of Göttingen, Germany, under the guidance of Max Born, he worked on the theoretical description of molecular electronic states. The Born-Oppenheimer Approximation allowed for the separation of the motion of atomic nuclei and electrons in molecules, significantly simplifying the quantum mechanical calculations of molecular systems. This approximation is widely used in quantum chemistry to this day.

Oppenheimer also conducted research on quantum tunneling, a phenomenon where particles can pass through potential barriers despite classical mechanics predicting the barrier to be impenetrable.

He made contributions to the understanding of the quantum mechanical behavior of particles in the context of nuclear reactions and radioactive decay. His work on quantum tunneling provided valuable insights into the behavior of subatomic particles and the probabilistic nature of quantum mechanics.

In collaboration with his student Melba Phillips, Oppenheimer developed the Oppenheimer-Phillips Process, a theoretical process that explained the creation of positron-electron pairs through the collision of high-energy photons with atomic nuclei. This work contributed to the understanding of particle production in high-energy interactions and had implications for the study of elementary particles.

Oppenheimer also explored the field of astrophysics and the nuclear processes occurring within stars. During the 1930s, he conducted research on stellar nucleosynthesis, the process by which elements are synthesized through nuclear reactions inside stars. His work laid the groundwork for understanding the origins of elements in the universe and their abundance in different stellar environments.

In the early 1930s, Oppenheimer worked on the theoretical prediction of black holes. In collaboration with Hartland Snyder, he investigated the gravitational collapse of massive stars and the formation of singularities, leading to the concept of black holes. Their research provided important insights into the astrophysical implications of general relativity and the end stages of stellar evolution.

Oppenheimer also made contributions to quantum field theory, a fundamental framework in theoretical physics that describes the behavior of elementary particles and their interactions. His work in this area contributed to the development of quantum electrodynamics (QED), a theory describing electromagnetic interactions between charged particles.

Beyond his specific research contributions, Oppenheimer was a prominent leader in the field of theoretical physics. He played a crucial role in fostering collaboration and exchange of ideas among physicists, particularly during his time as director of the Institute for Advanced Study in Princeton, New Jersey. Under his leadership, the Institute became a hub of theoretical physics research and attracted some of the brightest minds in the field.

SIGNIFICANT ACHIEVEMENTS BEFORE HIS INVOLVEMENT IN THE MANHATTAN PROJECT

Before his involvement in the Manhattan Project, J. Robert Oppenheimer had already established himself as a prominent and influential theoretical physicist. His significant achievements spanned various areas of physics and astrophysics, showcasing his intellectual prowess and innovative thinking. Here are some of his major achievements before the Manhattan Project:

Oppenheimer's early research focused on quantum mechanics, particularly in the context of molecular structure. His collaboration with Max Born at the University of Göttingen led to the development of the Born-Oppenheimer Approximation. This groundbreaking approximation simplified the quantum mechanical description of molecular systems by separating the motion of atomic nuclei and electrons, greatly advancing the field of quantum chemistry.

During the 1930s, Oppenheimer ventured into astrophysics and conducted research on stellar nucleosynthesis. He investigated the nuclear processes occurring within stars, shedding light on the origin of elements through nuclear reactions. His work laid the foundation for understanding the synthesis of elements in stars and the role of nucleosynthesis in shaping the chemical composition of the universe.

Oppenheimer's research also delved into the astrophysical implications of general relativity. In collaboration with Hartland Snyder, he explored the gravitational collapse of massive stars, leading to the prediction of black holes. Their work contributed significantly to the understanding of the end stages of stellar evolution and the formation of singularities.

.

CHAPTER 3

THE MANHATTAN PROJECT

The Manhattan Project was a top-secret research and development project undertaken during World War II by the United States, the United Kingdom, and Canada. Its primary objective was to develop the world's first atomic bomb, a powerful and devastating weapon that harnessed the energy released by nuclear fission. The project was named after the Manhattan Engineer District, a code name for the U.S. Army Corps of Engineers, which oversaw the project's management.

The origins of the Manhattan Project can be traced back to the discovery of nuclear fission in Germany in the late 1930s. Fearing that Nazi Germany might develop atomic weapons, a group of prominent scientists, including Albert Einstein and Leo Szilard, sent a letter to President Franklin D. Roosevelt in 1939, warning about the potential military implications of nuclear technology. This letter spurred the U.S. government to initiate research into nuclear fission and the development of atomic weapons.

Oppenheimer was appointed as the scientific director of the Manhattan Project in 1942. He played a crucial role in leading the team of scientists and engineers at the Los Alamos Laboratory, the primary site for the bomb's development. Other key figures included General Leslie R. Groves, who oversaw the overall project management, and physicist Richard Feynman, who made significant contributions to the project.

The Manhattan Project involved extensive research and development in various locations across the United States, including Los Alamos, New Mexico; Oak Ridge, Tennessee; and Hanford, Washington. Scientists and engineers worked tirelessly to overcome scientific and engineering challenges, including enriching uranium and producing plutonium, the two fissile materials required for the bomb.

OPPENHEIMER AS THE SCIENTIFIC DIRECTOR OF THE MANHATTAN PROJECT

The circumstances that led J. Robert Oppenheimer to become the scientific director of the Manhattan Project were a combination of his exceptional scientific expertise, his leadership skills, and the urgent need for a top-level scientist to lead the ambitious and secretive project during World War II

By the early 1940s, Oppenheimer had already established himself as one of the leading theoretical physicists of his time. His contributions to quantum mechanics, astrophysics, and quantum field theory had garnered him a reputation as a brilliant and innovative scientist. Oppenheimer's expertise made him an obvious choice for involvement in any scientific endeavor of great importance.

Prior to the Manhattan Project, Oppenheimer was associated with the University of California, Berkeley, where he held the position of professor of physics and conducted research at the Berkeley Radiation Laboratory. His previous work included some defense-related research, and he had shown an interest in the application of physics to national security.

The inception of the Manhattan Project was driven by fears that Nazi Germany might develop atomic weapons. In late 1941, physicist Karl T. Compton, acting as a representative of Vannevar Bush, the director of the Office of Scientific Research and Development (OSRD), approached Oppenheimer about participating in a secret defense project. Bush, who oversaw U.S. scientific research during the war, highly regarded Oppenheimer's scientific abilities and recommended him for a key role in the project.

Oppenheimer's background as a theoretical physicist and his familiarity with military defense work made him an ideal candidate to bridge the gap between the scientific community and the military. The Manhattan Project required close collaboration between scientists and military personnel to develop the atomic bomb successfully. Oppenheimer's ability to communicate complex scientific ideas to non-scientists made him a valuable asset in this regard.

EXPLORE THE CHALLENGES FACED DURING THE PROJECT

The Manhattan Project faced numerous challenges during its development, making it one of the most complex and high-stakes scientific endeavors in history. These challenges spanned scientific, technical, logistical, ethical, and security aspects. Here's an expanded exploration of the challenges faced during the project:

The development of the atomic bomb required groundbreaking research in nuclear physics, including the understanding of nuclear fission, the behavior of subatomic particles, and the properties of fissile materials like uranium-235 and plutonium-239. Scientists had to push the boundaries of existing knowledge and develop new theories to make the bomb a reality.

Creating an atomic bomb necessitated tackling numerous technical difficulties. Scientists and engineers had to design and build complex machinery to enrich uranium and produce plutonium in sufficient quantities. The creation of implosion devices and the design of bomb components were technically demanding tasks, requiring precise engineering and materials.

Enriching uranium to obtain the required amount of fissile isotope uranium-235 was a significant challenge. Scientists and engineers had to develop sophisticated methods like gaseous diffusion, electromagnetic separation, and the centrifuge process to increase the concentration of uranium-235.

Producing sufficient quantities of plutonium-239 was equally challenging. The production of plutonium required large-scale nuclear reactors and intricate processes to extract and purify the plutonium from irradiated nuclear fuel.

The Manhattan Project was conducted during World War II, and there was immense time pressure to develop the bomb before Germany or other hostile nations could achieve the same breakthrough. The urgency to complete the project and achieve a successful test added significant stress and demanded optimal use of resources.

Maintaining strict security and secrecy was critical for the success of the project. The development of the atomic bomb was classified top-secret, and scientists and workers involved were not fully aware of the overall objective. Security measures were implemented to prevent leaks of sensitive information and to safeguard against espionage.

The Manhattan Project raised profound ethical and moral dilemmas. Scientists and engineers were aware of the destructive potential of the atomic bomb, and the project's success meant developing a weapon of unprecedented power. Balancing the imperative to win the war with the potential consequences of using such a weapon raised ethical questions for those involved.

The development of nuclear weapons came with inherent safety risks. Researchers and workers had to handle dangerous materials and work with equipment that posed radiation hazards. Safety protocols had to be carefully developed and adhered to.

CHAPTER 4

THE ATOMIC BOMBINGS AND AFTERMATH

IMPACT OF THE SUCCESSFUL DEVELOPMENT

The successful development and use of the atomic bomb during World War II had far-reaching and multifaceted consequences that profoundly impacted various aspects of history, science, geopolitics, and society

The most immediate and significant impact of the atomic bombings was the end of World War II. The bombings of Hiroshima and Nagasaki in August 1945 forced Japan's surrender, bringing a swift conclusion to the war. The devastation caused by the bombings, coupled with the fear of further atomic attacks, left Japan in a state of shock and contributed to the decision to surrender.

The atomic bombings marked the beginning of the nuclear age, a new era characterized by the development and proliferation of nuclear weapons. The successful detonation of the atomic bombs demonstrated the immense destructive power of nuclear technology, and it sparked a global race among nations to acquire nuclear weapons for military deterrence and security reasons.

The atomic bombings intensified the rivalry between the United States and the Soviet Union, leading to the Cold War. Both superpowers sought to expand their nuclear arsenals, and the fear of a nuclear conflict loomed large. This ideological standoff shaped global politics for several decades, with each side engaging in nuclear brinkmanship to maintain a balance of power.

The successful development of the atomic bomb motivated other countries to seek nuclear weapons for their own security. The United Kingdom, France, China, and later India, Pakistan, and North Korea, among others, joined the nuclear club, increasing concerns about nuclear proliferation and the risk of nuclear conflict.

The use of atomic bombs raised profound ethical and moral questions about the use of weapons of mass destruction. Many critics argued that the bombings violated principles of just war and proportionality, leading to debates about the morality of using such devastating weapons against civilian populations.

The Manhattan Project's success accelerated advancements in nuclear technology. The knowledge gained during the project laid the groundwork for the peaceful use of nuclear energy. Nuclear power plants were later developed for civilian purposes, providing a significant source of electricity in many countries.

The devastation caused by the atomic bombings instilled a deep fear of nuclear warfare in the global consciousness. The concept of nuclear deterrence emerged, whereby the possession of nuclear weapons was believed to prevent large-scale conflicts due to the fear of mutually assured destruction.

The atomic bombings had a lasting impact on Japanese society. The immediate death and suffering caused by the bombings were immense, and the survivors (hibakusha) faced long-term health issues and social stigma. The bombings influenced Japan's post-war pacifist stance and commitment to promoting global nuclear disarmament.

HIROSHIMA AND NAGASAKI

The use of the atomic bomb on the Japanese cities of Hiroshima and Nagasaki during World War II remains one of the most controversial and debated events in history.

By mid-1945, World War II was nearing its end, but Japan showed no signs of surrender. The Allies, led by the United States, were seeking a swift conclusion to the war to prevent further loss of life and to secure victory.

The Pacific Theater of the war had been particularly brutal, with fierce resistance from Japanese forces on multiple fronts. The Battle of Okinawa, for instance, saw heavy casualties on both sides and reinforced the notion that invading Japan would lead to significant loss of life.

U.S. military planners believed that a direct invasion of Japan would likely result in massive casualties for both American and Japanese forces. The projected death toll for a full-scale invasion was a major factor in considering alternatives to force Japan's surrender.

On August 6, 1945, the U.S. B-29 bomber "Enola Gay" dropped the first atomic bomb, code-named "Little Boy," on the city of Hiroshima. The bomb's explosion resulted in massive destruction, killing an estimated 140,000 people by the end of 1945.

Three days later, on August 9, 1945, a second atomic bomb, code-named "Fat Man," was dropped on Nagasaki. The bomb claimed the lives of approximately 70,000 people by the end of 1945.

The bombings had a decisive impact on Japan's decision to surrender. On August 15, 1945, Emperor Hirohito announced Japan's acceptance of the terms of the Potsdam Declaration, effectively ending the war.

The bombings caused immense human suffering and loss of life. The immediate and long-term effects of the radiation resulted in high casualty figures and lasting health issues for survivors (hibakusha).

After the war, Japan faced the monumental task of rebuilding its devastated cities and infrastructure. In the aftermath, Japan pursued a path of peace and reconciliation with its neighbors, eventually becoming a leading advocate for disarmament and nuclear non-proliferation.

OPPENHEIMER'S FEELINGS AND THOUGHTS ABOUT THE BOMB'S USE

J. Robert Oppenheimer, who was the scientific director of the Manhattan Project, had complex feelings and thoughts about the use of the atomic bomb and the ethical dilemmas it presented. As the project progressed and the devastating potential of the bomb became evident, Oppenheimer grappled with the profound moral implications of his work.

Oppenheimer understood the immense responsibility he bore as the leader of the Manhattan Project and one of the architects of the atomic bomb. He was well aware of the weapon's unprecedented destructive power and the potential loss of innocent lives associated with its use.

As the project reached its culmination, Oppenheimer experienced moral ambivalence about the bomb's use. On the one hand, he recognized the urgent need to bring the war to an end and prevent further loss of life on both sides. On the other hand, he grappled with the immense human cost and suffering that the bomb would inflict on the civilian populations of Hiroshima and Nagasaki.

Oppenheimer feared that the successful use of the atomic bomb might open the door to unlimited warfare in the future. The bomb's devastating impact could potentially lead to a cycle of escalation, where nations might increasingly resort to nuclear weapons in conflicts.

In the aftermath of the bombings, Oppenheimer's reflections on the ethical implications of the bomb's use deepened. He expressed regret for his role in the development of nuclear weapons and became an advocate for nuclear arms control and disarmament.

After the war, Oppenheimer became involved in efforts to promote international control and cooperation on nuclear issues. He advocated for the establishment of international organizations to oversee nuclear technology and prevent nuclear proliferation.

CHAPTER 5

POST-WAR CAREER AND CONTROVERSIES

OPPENHEIMER'S WORK AFTER WORLD WAR II

After World War II, J. Robert Oppenheimer's career took a different trajectory as he transitioned from his role in the development of the atomic bomb to become a prominent figure in academia and scientific research. Oppenheimer was appointed as chairman of the General Advisory Committee (GAC) of the newly established United States Atomic Energy Commission (AEC) in 1946. In this capacity, he played a key role in shaping the nation's post-war nuclear policy, including recommendations for the civilian control of nuclear energy and the international control of atomic weapons.

In 1947, Oppenheimer accepted an appointment as the Director of the Institute for Advanced Study in Princeton, New Jersey. The IAS was an esteemed academic institution where leading scholars from various fields could pursue research independently of teaching duties. As Director, Oppenheimer was tasked with overseeing the institute's operations and fostering an environment conducive to cutting-edge research.

Throughout his tenure at the Institute for Advanced Study, Oppenheimer continued his research in theoretical physics. He made significant contributions to quantum mechanics, astrophysics, and quantum field theory. His work in these areas solidified his reputation as a brilliant physicist and a leading figure in the field.

As Director of the IAS, Oppenheimer played a crucial role in mentoring and supporting young scientists. He created an intellectually stimulating environment, attracting some of the brightest minds in the scientific community. His guidance and mentorship had a lasting impact on many scientists who later became influential figures in their own right.

While Oppenheimer was highly respected for his scientific contributions, his political past and associations during the war also attracted scrutiny. He faced accusations of being a security risk and having communist sympathies during the Second Red Scare, leading to a highly controversial security clearance hearing in 1954.

During the security clearance hearing, Oppenheimer's loyalty and character were questioned, and his clearance was ultimately revoked. The fallout from this hearing and the political climate at the time had a detrimental impact on his career and personal life. Despite the negative outcome, he continued to be respected by the scientific community.

After his departure from the Institute for Advanced Study in 1952, Oppenheimer served as a consultant to various scientific organizations. He remained active in advocating for arms control and international cooperation on nuclear issues. He spoke out against the further development and proliferation of nuclear weapons and advocated for peaceful uses of nuclear energy.

EVENTS SURROUNDING THE REVOCATION OF HIS SECURITY CLEARANCE

The revocation of J. Robert Oppenheimer's security clearance and the controversies that followed were significant events that had a profound impact on his personal and professional life. These events stemmed from concerns about his political associations and loyalty during a period of heightened anti-communist sentiment in the United States

In the early 1950s, during the Second Red Scare and the McCarthy era, suspicions arose regarding Oppenheimer's past associations with left-leaning individuals and organizations, including his involvement with communist and progressive groups in the 1930s. Additionally, his past associations with scientists who were later identified as having communist ties added to the concerns.

Oppenheimer was accused of being a security risk and having communist sympathies. His critics contended that his political leanings and past associations could make him susceptible to providing sensitive information to potential enemies or obstructing national security efforts.

In 1953, the AEC formed a Personnel Security Board, also known as the Gray Board, to review Oppenheimer's security clearance. The board conducted extensive investigations into his background and associations.

During the hearing, Oppenheimer faced intense questioning about his past associations and political beliefs. He cooperated with the investigation but refused to divulge certain confidential information, asserting that he had safeguarded national security during the war.

In June 1954, the Gray Board concluded that Oppenheimer's security clearance should be revoked. The AEC's chairman, Lewis Strauss, accepted the board's recommendation, and in a controversial decision, he revoked Oppenheimer's clearance, effectively barring him from accessing classified information.

The decision to revoke Oppenheimer's security clearance sparked a storm of public debate and controversy. Many prominent scientists, including Albert Einstein, voiced their support for Oppenheimer, arguing that the decision was unjust and could have a chilling effect on scientific research and intellectual freedom.

The revocation of his security clearance had a profound impact on Oppenheimer's career and reputation. He became a lightning rod for criticism and was ostracized from government-related scientific activities. Despite the setback, he remained active in scientific research and continued to advocate for arms control and peaceful uses of nuclear energy.

CHAPTER 6

PERSONAL LIFE AND LEGACY

PERSONAL LIFE AND INTERESTS

J. Robert Oppenheimer's personal life and interests were as intriguing as his scientific achievements. Beyond his groundbreaking work in physics, Oppenheimer's life was filled with a myriad of passions and pursuits.

Oppenheimer had a profound love for literature and poetry. He was well-read and had a remarkable ability to quote passages from classic works and religious texts. He often incorporated literary references into his speeches and writings, showcasing his appreciation for the power of words and language.

Oppenheimer was highly proficient in multiple languages. Besides his native English, he was fluent in French, German, and Sanskrit. His linguistic prowess allowed him to engage with foreign literature and philosophical texts, contributing to his wide-ranging intellectual interests.

Oppenheimer had a keen eye for art and enjoyed collecting works of renowned artists. He particularly admired modern art and owned pieces by celebrated painters like Pablo Picasso and Diego Rivera. Additionally, he had a love for classical music and was known to play the piano. Attending concerts and performances brought him joy and relaxation.

Apart from his scientific endeavors, Oppenheimer was known for his insatiable intellectual curiosity. He explored various disciplines, including history, philosophy, and political theory. His fascination with the world beyond physics allowed him to have stimulating discussions with colleagues from diverse fields.

Oppenheimer found solace and inspiration in nature. He frequently engaged in outdoor activities such as hiking and horseback riding, particularly during his time in New Mexico, where he worked at Los Alamos National Laboratory. The stunning landscapes of the region provided him with moments of reflection and contemplation.

While Oppenheimer was dedicated to his work and the seriousness of scientific pursuits, he was also known for his wit and sense of humor. He used humor as a means of connecting with colleagues and breaking tension during difficult periods.

FAMILY LIFE

J. Robert Oppenheimer's family life was a mix of personal joys and challenges, closely intertwined with his illustrious scientific career.

Oppenheimer married Katherine "Kitty" Puening Harrison in 1940. They had two children together: Peter and Katherine. Despite the demands of Oppenheimer's work and the challenges they faced, their marriage was a significant part of his life.

Oppenheimer's demanding work schedule, particularly during the Manhattan Project, often took him away from his family for extended periods. This created strains on his marriage and led to periods of emotional distance between him and his wife.

The immense responsibility and pressure associated with the development of the atomic bomb also affected Oppenheimer emotionally. He carried the weight of the project's success and consequences, which influenced his interactions with family members.

Despite the challenges they faced, Kitty remained supportive of Oppenheimer throughout his career. She understood the significance of his work and the demands it placed on him. Kitty provided a stable and supportive home environment for their children.

The tragic death of Oppenheimer's younger brother, Frank, by suicide in 1939, deeply impacted him and his family. The loss had a lasting effect on Oppenheimer's emotional well-being and shaped his outlook on life.

After his brother's death, Oppenheimer and Kitty adopted their nephew, Robert Harrison, providing him with a loving and nurturing home. This act of familial responsibility demonstrated their commitment to family bonds.

The political controversies and the revocation of Oppenheimer's security clearance took a toll on his personal life. The strain from the security clearance hearing and its aftermath further complicated his family dynamics.

Throughout his life, Oppenheimer relied on a network of close friends and colleagues who offered emotional support during challenging times. These friendships provided him with valuable connections outside his professional realm.

RELATIONSHIPS WITH COLLEAGUES

J. Robert Oppenheimer's relationships with colleagues were marked by both admiration and complexity. As a prominent physicist and leader in the scientific community, Oppenheimer interacted with a diverse group of individuals who played significant roles in his professional and personal life.

Oppenheimer was known for his exceptional leadership and collaboration skills. He worked closely with a wide array of physicists, mathematicians, and other scientists on various projects. His ability to foster a collaborative atmosphere allowed for groundbreaking advancements in theoretical physics.

As a mentor, Oppenheimer was highly influential in shaping the careers of young scientists. He encouraged and supported their intellectual growth and provided guidance to aspiring researchers, ensuring a new generation of physicists was well-prepared for their scientific pursuits.

Oppenheimer shared a particularly close friendship with Niels Bohr, the Danish physicist. They engaged in extensive scientific discussions and corresponded frequently on topics ranging from quantum mechanics to the implications of nuclear weapons. Oppenheimer respected Bohr's intellect and valued his insights.

Oppenheimer's relationship with physicist Edward Teller was fraught with tension. Teller had a different approach to scientific research and national security issues, which clashed with Oppenheimer's perspectives. Tensions between the two escalated during the Manhattan Project and continued in the aftermath.

Oppenheimer's brilliance and passion for scientific inquiry had a profound impact on his colleagues. His ability to think deeply and approach complex problems inspired those around him and influenced the way they approached scientific research.

Oppenheimer was renowned for his keen intellect and was often sought after for intellectual discussions. His colleagues admired his depth of knowledge and appreciated the opportunity to engage in stimulating debates with him.

Oppenheimer's political controversies during the Second Red Scare also affected his relationships with some colleagues. Some scientists were critical of his past associations and political views, while others staunchly defended him against the accusations.

LASTING IMPACT OF HIS CONTRIBUTIONS TO SCIENCE

J. Robert Oppenheimer's contributions to science, nuclear physics, and the world have left a lasting impact that continues to shape our understanding of the universe, nuclear energy, and the ethical implications of scientific discovery. As one of the leading figures in 20th-century physics, Oppenheimer's legacy extends beyond his pivotal role in the development of the atomic bomb

Oppenheimer made significant contributions to theoretical physics, particularly in the fields of quantum mechanics and astrophysics. His work in quantum theory laid the foundation for understanding the behavior of subatomic particles, and his research in astrophysics advanced our understanding of stellar processes and the evolution of stars.

Oppenheimer's leadership as the scientific director of the Manhattan Project was instrumental in the successful development of the atomic bomb during World War II. The project's success revolutionized nuclear physics and ushered in the nuclear age. While the use of atomic weapons in Hiroshima and Nagasaki remains a subject of ethical debate, the Manhattan Project's scientific achievements demonstrated the immense power and potential risks of nuclear energy.

The atomic bomb's successful development had far-reaching consequences on global politics and national security. The advent of nuclear weapons changed the dynamics of international relations and led to the Cold War between the United States and the Soviet Union. The concept of nuclear deterrence and the delicate balance of power between nuclear-armed nations became key elements of international politics.

After World War II, Oppenheimer shifted his focus to advocating for arms control and peaceful uses of nuclear energy. He was a vocal proponent of international cooperation to prevent nuclear proliferation and the spread of nuclear weapons. His influential voice added weight to calls for arms control agreements and treaties, emphasizing the importance of responsible scientific stewardship.

Oppenheimer's involvement in the atomic bomb project led him to confront profound ethical dilemmas concerning the impact of scientific discoveries on humanity. The experience influenced his perspectives on the responsible use of scientific knowledge and the potential consequences of unchecked technological advancements. His reflections on the moral implications of scientific research have had a lasting impact on discussions surrounding the responsible conduct of science.

Beyond his work in nuclear physics, Oppenheimer's research in astrophysics laid the groundwork for subsequent studies of stellar processes and the behavior of celestial bodies. His contributions have continued to influence our understanding of the universe and have informed space exploration missions and the study of cosmic phenomena.

CONCLUSION

KEY POINTS OF J. ROBERT OPPENHEIMER'S LIFE

Early Life and Education: Born on April 22, 1904, Oppenheimer showed early signs of brilliance and a passion for literature and science. He pursued degrees at Harvard and the University of Göttingen, where he developed a deep interest in theoretical physics and quantum mechanics.

Scientific Contributions: Oppenheimer made significant contributions to theoretical physics and astrophysics, laying the groundwork for our understanding of quantum behavior and stellar processes.

Manhattan Project: As the scientific director of the Manhattan Project during World War II, Oppenheimer led the successful development of the atomic bomb. The project's success marked the beginning of the nuclear age and had a profound impact on global politics and national security.

Ethical Dilemmas: Oppenheimer's involvement in the atomic bomb project led to ethical reflections on the responsible use of scientific knowledge and the consequences of unchecked technological advancements.

Advocacy for Peaceful Uses of Nuclear Energy: After the war, Oppenheimer became an advocate for arms control and the peaceful uses of nuclear energy, emphasizing international cooperation to prevent nuclear proliferation.

Mentorship and Influence: Oppenheimer's mentorship and leadership in the scientific community influenced future generations of scientists, fostering an environment of intellectual curiosity and collaboration.

Security Clearance Controversy: Oppenheimer's security clearance was controversially revoked during the Second Red Scare, raising concerns about the intersection of politics and science.

SIGNIFICANCE AND THE LESSONS THAT CAN BE LEARNED FROM HIS LIFE STORY

J. Robert Oppenheimer's life story is one of immense significance, fraught with scientific achievements, ethical dilemmas, and complex human experiences. His legacy offers several valuable lessons that resonate with individuals across various fields and periods of history. Here are some reflections on Oppenheimer's significance and the lessons that can be learned from his life:

The Power of Human Ingenuity:

Oppenheimer's contributions to theoretical physics and the successful development of the atomic bomb demonstrate the power of human ingenuity and intellect. His work showcased the potential of scientific discovery to shape the course of history and transform our understanding of the universe.

Ethical Considerations in Scientific Pursuits:

The ethical dilemmas faced by Oppenheimer during the Manhattan Project underscore the importance of considering the potential consequences of scientific discoveries. His reflections on the responsible use of scientific knowledge serve as a poignant reminder of the moral dimensions that accompany groundbreaking advancements.

The Intersection of Science and Society:

Oppenheimer's life story highlights the complex and often delicate relationship between science and society. His involvement in the Manhattan Project exemplifies the profound impact scientific research can have on global politics and national security. His experiences underscore the need for responsible scientific stewardship and open dialogue between scientists, policymakers, and the public.

The Fragility of Human Progress:

Despite his brilliance and achievements, Oppenheimer faced personal and professional challenges, including controversies surrounding his security clearance. His life story reminds us that human progress is not immune to setbacks, political pressures, and individual vulnerabilities.

The Role of Mentorship and Collaboration:

Oppenheimer's mentorship and collaboration with colleagues exemplify the importance of fostering a supportive and intellectually stimulating environment for the next generation of scientists. His willingness to share knowledge and ideas contributed to the growth and success of many young researchers.

The Pursuit of Peace and International Cooperation:

After World War II, Oppenheimer became an advocate for arms control and peaceful uses of nuclear energy. His commitment to international cooperation and preventing nuclear proliferation underscores the necessity of seeking diplomatic solutions to global challenges.

Embracing a Multifaceted Life:

Oppenheimer's diverse interests in literature, art, music, and philosophy exemplify the richness of a multifaceted life. His ability to engage with different disciplines demonstrates the value of pursuing intellectual curiosity beyond one's primary field of expertise.

Lessons from Controversy:

The controversies surrounding Oppenheimer's life highlight the importance of safeguarding scientific freedom and the principles of academic freedom. His story serves as a cautionary tale about the potential consequences of conflating scientific inquiry with political ideologies.

Printed in Great Britain
by Amazon

25747610R00030